DATE DUE

A Note from
Mary Pope Osborne About the

MAGIC TREE HOUSE®

FACT TRACKERS

When I write Magic Tree House® adventures, I love including facts about the times and places Jack and Annie visit. But when readers finish these adventures, I want them to learn even more. So that's why my husband, Will, and my sister, Natalie Pope Boyce, and I write a series of nonfiction books that are companions to the fiction titles in the Magic Tree House® series. We call these books Fact Trackers because we love to track the facts! Whether we're researching dinosaurs, pyramids, Pilgrims, sea monsters, or cobras, we're always amazed at how wondrous and surprising the real world is. We want you to experience the same wonder we do—so get out your pencils and notebooks and hit the trail with us. You can be a Magic Tree House® Fact Tracker, too!

Mary Pope Osborne

Here's what kids, parents, and teachers have to say about the Magic Tree House® Fact Trackers:

"They are so good. I can't wait for the next one. All I can say for now is prepare to be amazed!" —Alexander N.

"I have read every Magic Tree House book there is. The [Fact Trackers] are a thrilling way to get more information about the special events in the story." —John R.

"These are fascinating nonfiction books that enhance the magical time-traveling adventures of Jack and Annie. I love these books, especially *American Revolution*. I was learning so much, and I didn't even know it!" —Tori Beth S.

"[They] are an excellent 'behind-the-scenes' look at what the [Magic Tree House fiction] has started in your imagination! You can't buy one without the other; they are such a complement to one another." —Erika N., mom

"Magic Tree House [Fact Trackers] took my children on a journey from Frog Creek, Pennsylvania, to so many significant historical events! The detailed manuals are a remarkable addition to the classic fiction Magic Tree House books we adore!" —Jenny S., mom

"[They] are very useful tools in my classroom, as they allow for students to be part of the planning process. Together, we find facts in the [Fact Trackers] to extend the learning introduced in the fictional companions. Researching and planning classroom activities, such as our class Olympics based on facts found in *Ancient Greece and the Olympics*, help create a genuine love for learning!" —Paula H., teacher

Magic Tree House®
Fact Tracker

RAIN FORESTS

A nonfiction companion to
Magic Tree House® #6:
Afternoon on the Amazon

by Will Osborne
and Mary Pope Osborne

illustrated by Sal Murdocca

A STEPPING STONE BOOK™
Random House New York

Text copyright © 2001 by Will Osborne and Mary Pope Osborne
Illustrations copyright © 2001 by Sal Murdocca
Cover photograph copyright © Steve Winterings/NGS Image Collection

The Magic Tree House Fact Tracker series was formerly known as the
Magic Tree House Research Guide series.

Visit us on the Web!
MagicTreeHouse.com
www.randomhouse.com/kids

Educators and librarians, for a variety of teaching tools, visit us at
www.randomhouse.com/teachers

Library of Congress Cataloging-in-Publication Data
Osborne, Will.
Rain forests : a nonfiction companion to Magic tree house #6,
Afternoon on the Amazon / by Will Osborne and Mary Pope Osborne ;
illustrated by Sal Murdocca.
    p. cm. — (Magic tree house fact tracker) (A stepping stone book)
Includes index.
ISBN 978-0-375-81355-9 (trade) — ISBN 978-0-375-91355-6 (lib. bdg.)
1. Rain forests—Juvenile literature. I. Osborne, Mary Pope. II. Murdocca, Sal,
ill. III. Title. IV. Series.
QK938.R34 O83 2011 577.34—dc22 2011009616

Printed in the United States of America
10 9 8 7 6 5

For Shana Corey

Scientific Consultant:

DR. ANNETTE AIELLO, Staff Scientist, Smithsonian Tropical Research Institute, Panama

Anthropological Consultant:

DR. OLGA LINARES, Staff Scientist, Smithsonian Tropical Research Institute, Panama

Education Consultant:

MELINDA MURPHY, Media Specialist, Reed Elementary School, Cypress Fairbanks Independent School District, Houston, Texas

We would also like to thank Paul Coughlin for his ongoing photographic contribution to the series and, again, our wonderful, creative team at Random House: Joanne Yates, Helena Winston, Diane Landolf, Cathy Goldsmith, Mallory Loehr, and, of course, our wonderful editor, Shana Corey.

RAIN FORESTS

Contents

Dear Readers,

When we traveled through the Amazon Rain Forest in <u>Afternoon on the Amazon</u>, we learned that rain forests are amazing places. But we didn't really understand <u>how</u> amazing they are until we got back to Frog Creek!

We discovered that lots of things we use every day come from rain forests around the world. We learned that there are more different kinds of plants and animals in rain forests than anywhere else on earth. And we learned lots of reasons why it's really important to keep the rain forests of the world from being destroyed.

How did we learn all these things? We tracked down the facts!

We went to the library and checked out rain forest books. We found rain forest websites. We rented a video about rain forest animals at our local video store. We took notes and drew pictures. Then we shared what we learned with our parents and teachers and friends.

Now we want to share our research with you. So get your notebook, get your backpack, and get ready to explore the incredible world of rain forests!

Jack

Annie

1

What Is a Rain Forest?

Rain forests are rich and wonderful worlds. They are filled with tall trees, strange animals, giant bugs, and amazing plants. The largest flowers in the world grow in rain forests. The smallest frogs and the biggest spiders live in rain forests, too.

A few rain forests have a short dry season when it doesn't rain at all. They are called <u>seasonal forests</u>.

There are rain forests all around the world. Each rain forest has different kinds of plants and creatures living in it. But most rain forests are alike in several ways:

1. Rain forests get <u>lots</u> of rain.

That's why we call them *rain* forests! In most rain forests, it rains nearly every day. Often there are thunderstorms.

Nearly all rain forests get over six feet of rain per year. Many get more than *sixteen* feet of rain—and some get as much as *thirty*!

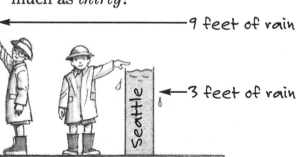

We think of Seattle, Washington, as a very rainy city. But Seattle only gets about three feet of rain per year!

2. Rain forests have very high <u>humidity</u>.

Humidity (hyoo-MID-uh-tee) is the amount of moisture in the air. Even when it isn't raining, the air in a rain forest feels wet and steamy.

Water Cycle of a Rain Forest

Moist air forms clouds.

Rain falls.

Water released into air.

Roots soak up moisture.

3. Rain forests are very warm.

The temperature in most rain forests stays between 75 and 80 degrees all year long.

4. In most rain forests, there isn't much difference between winter and summer.

The temperature is warm and the humidity is almost always high.

Rain Forest
Lots of rain

High humidity

Warm temperature

Weather stays the same

Tropical Rain Forests

Most rain forests are *tropical forests*. That means they grow near an imaginary line that runs all the way around the middle of the earth. This line is called the *equator* (ih-KWAY-tur).

The biggest tropical rain forest is the Amazon Rain Forest in South America (see the map on pages 18 and 19). The Amazon Rain Forest is bigger than the states of Texas, California, Colorado, Florida, Nevada, Arizona, Oregon, Minnesota, and Alaska combined!

There are also large tropical rain forests in Central America, Africa, Asia, New Guinea, Australia, and many islands in the Pacific Ocean.

More different kinds of animals, insects, and plants live in tropical rain forests than anywhere else on earth!

17

Rain Forests Around the World

NORTH AMERICA

Atlantic Ocean

AFRICA

CENTRAL AMERICA

Equator

Pacific Ocean

SOUTH AMERICA

18

2

✹

Layers of a Tropical Rain Forest

A tropical rain forest is like a building with several different floors. The "floors" are called *strata* (STRA-tuh), or *layers*. Each layer is home for different kinds of plants and creatures.

The Canopy
The tops of the trees in a forest form a layer called the *canopy* (KAN-uh-pee).

The canopy is like a big green umbrella over the whole forest. In most tropical rain forests, the canopy is more than a hundred feet above the ground!

The canopy is noisy! Most of the animals of the rain forest live there. Birds squawk, monkeys chatter, and frogs croak all day long. They feed on canopy leaves, insects,

You can hear a howler monkey howl from three miles away!

Howler monkey

nuts, and fruits. Many animals live their whole lives in the canopy without ever touching the ground.

In some rain forests, a few trees grow even taller than the canopy trees. These trees are called *emergents* (ih-MUR-junts). The distance from the ground to the top of an emergent can be greater than the height of a fourteen-story building.

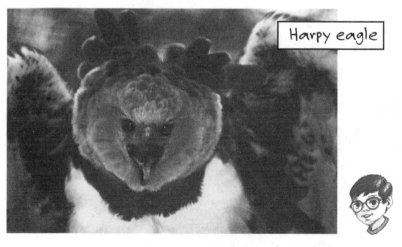

Harpy eagle

Harpy eagles live in emergent trees in Central and South American rain forests.

23

The Understory

Beneath the canopy and the emergents is a layer called the *understory* (UN-dur-stor-ee). The understory is dark and shadowy. That's because the leaves of the canopy are so close together that only a tiny bit of sun shines through.

The trees in the understory are not very tall. Some are young trees that will grow to become part of the canopy. But most understory trees never grow taller than about fifteen feet.

Ocelot

Several different kinds of wild cats live in the understory. The understory is also home for all sorts of bats, owls, monkeys, snakes, and lizards.

Ocelots look like beautiful house cats—only twice as big!

The Forest Floor

The bottom layer of a rain forest is the *forest floor*. The forest floor is very dark and quiet. The ground is covered with rotting leaves. A few ferns and bushes grow among the giant trunks of the canopy trees.

The animals that live on the forest floor are not nearly as noisy as those in the canopy and the understory. Jaguars prowl silently, looking for food. Snakes slither over tree roots. Millions of insects and

Layers of a Rain Forest

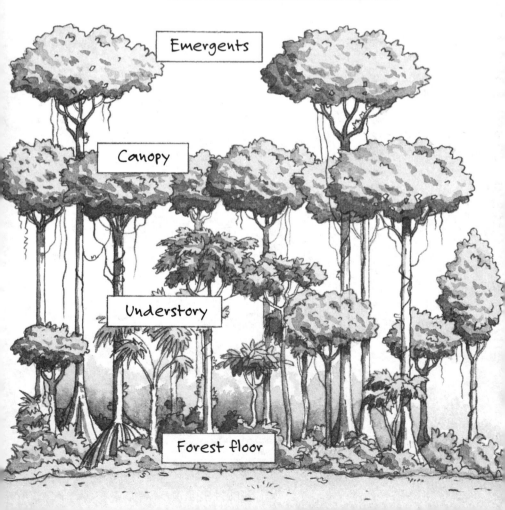

Emergents

Canopy

Understory

Forest floor

spiders creep through the carpet of dead leaves.

Each layer of a rain forest can seem like a separate world. But all the plants and animals in a rain forest are connected. They depend on each other to survive. This is called *interdependence* (in-tur-duh-PEN-dunts).

Turn the page to see an example of rain forest interdependence at work.

This way

The Interdependence of Fig Trees, Fig Wasps, Monkeys, Bats, and Birds

1. Tiny fig wasps lay their eggs in fig tree flowers. The wasps carry *pollen* from the flowers of other fig trees.

Pollen is the name for the tiny yellow or white grains inside most flowers.

2. Pollen causes the flowers the wasps have laid their eggs in to produce fruits. The fruits are full of fig seeds.

3. Monkeys, bats, and birds eat the fruits and spread the seeds to other parts of the forest.

4. New fig trees grow where seeds are dropped.

3

Rain Forest Plants

More than half of all the different kinds of plants on earth grow in rain forests. Many rain forest plants have not even been discovered or named yet. But some that we *do* know about are truly amazing!

There are plants that eat insects. There are plants with fruits longer than baseball bats. There are plants with flowers bigger than bicycle tires!

Giant rafflesia flower

Epiphytes

Many rain forest plants are *epiphytes* (EP-uh-fites). Epiphytes grow on trees or other plants. They have roots that never touch the ground.

Most rain forest epiphytes grow high on the trees of the canopy, where there is plenty of sunlight. One rain forest tree can have more than fifty different kinds of epiphytes growing on it.

Rain forest orchid

Nearly all orchids are epiphytes. There are over 20,000 different kinds of orchids in the rain forests of the world.

Vines

There are also lots of *vines* in the rain forest canopy and understory. Vines have roots in the ground, but climb up the trunks of trees to reach the sunlight.

Many rain forest vines have hard, woody stems. These vines are called *lianas* (lee-ANN-uhz). Some lianas have stems so thick that they look like twisted trees.

Liana

This liana is sometimes called a monkey ladder.

33

Rain forest lianas often loop from tree to tree. The lianas and branches of the canopy and understory make it easy for monkeys, squirrels, and other animals to travel through the forest.

Orangutan

Many of the plants that grow in the understory and on the forest floor have HUGE leaves!

Big leaves help these plants take in as much of the shadowy light as possible.

Fungi

Some plants don't need sunlight to grow. These plants are called *fungi* (FUN-jy).

Mushrooms and toadstools are fungi.

Shelf fungi

Fungi live off dead plant and animal matter. Many kinds of fungi grow on the trunks of dead trees and on the shady forest floor.

Turn the page to learn more about some of our favorite rain forest plants.

This way

Our Favorite Rain Forest Plants

Tropical Pitcher Plant

Special parts of these tropical vines grow in the shape of pitchers. The pitchers collect water when it rains.

The pitchers on tropical pitcher plants have a smell that attracts insects. They're also very slippery! When an insect lands on the rim of one of the pitchers, it slips down into the water inside. The insect drowns—and the pitcher plant uses it for food to help it grow.

Tropical pitcher plants grow in Southeast Asia and Australia.

38

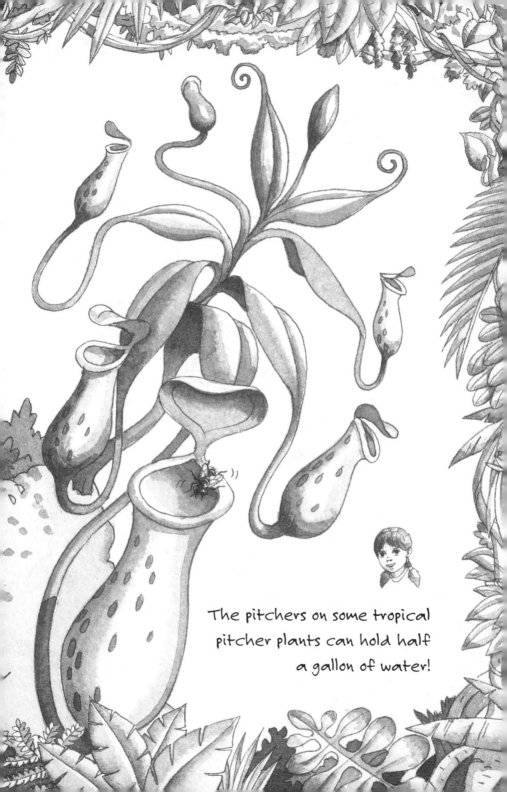

The pitchers on some tropical
pitcher plants can hold half
a gallon of water!

Giant rafflesias grow in the rain forests of Asia.

Giant Rafflesia

The giant rafflesia (ruh-FLEE-zee-uh) is the biggest flower in the world. The flower blooms on the forest floor. But the rest of the rafflesia plant is hidden underground.

Some giant rafflesia flowers are three feet across! They can weigh up to twenty-five pounds. That's heavier than a beagle!

Most flowers smell sweet. But the giant rafflesia stinks! It smells like rotten meat.

Sausage Tree

Sausage trees have beautiful red flowers. The flowers bloom at sunset and last for only one night. During the night, bats come to feed on the *nectar* and pollen of the flowers. The flowers hang from long, thin stalks so the bats can visit them easily.

Nectar is a liquid found in flowers.

When the flowers drop off in the morning, huge fruits start to grow in their place. The fruits can grow to be three feet long. When they're ripe, the tree looks as if it's covered with giant sausages!

Sausage trees grow in the
rain forests of Africa.

43

Strangler figs grow
in the rain forests
of Asia, South
America, and
Africa.

Strangler Fig

A strangler fig begins life as a liana, but later becomes a tree!

A strangler fig first begins to grow high in a canopy tree where monkeys, birds, or bats have dropped seeds. It sends leafy shoots to the top of the tree to soak up sunlight. At the same time, it sends roots down the tree trunk toward the ground.

When the roots reach the ground, they grow thicker and stronger. They begin to form a trunk of their own. The new trunk completely surrounds the tree the strangler fig has been growing on.

Eventually, the old tree dies and rots away. The strangler fig has stolen its place in the forest!

Strangler figs that grow in Africa are called <u>wonderbooms</u>.

Red colobus monkeys

4

Rain Forest Creatures

They creep and crawl! They flit and fly! They growl and howl! The world's rain forests are alive with millions of animals, bugs, and birds.

Predators and Protection

Most rain forest animals depend on other animals for food. Animals that kill and eat other animals are called *predators*. The animals that predators kill are called their *prey*.

47

Many rain forest creatures have special ways of protecting themselves from predators. Some have colors that help them blend with their natural surroundings. This kind of protection is called *camouflage* (KAM-uh-flahzh).

Lizards like this gecko (GEK-o) have skin that looks like rocks and dirt.

Some creatures fool predators by looking like plants. If they stay very still, predators will leave them alone—because they won't see them!

48

Insects like this katydid have wings
that look just like leaves.

Stick insects look just like twigs.

49

Some creatures scare predators away by looking bigger and scarier than they really are. Many moths and butterflies have marks on their wings that look like big eyes. When these creatures open their wings, predators think the eyes belong to a creature that might eat *them*!

Io moth

Marks like these are called <u>eyespots</u>.

Yikes!
Predators use camouflage, too. This vine snake looks more like a vine than a snake—until it attacks its prey!

Night Creatures

The rain forest is just as alive at night as it is during the day. Many creatures come out only after the sun has gone down. They are called *nocturnal* (nok-TUR-nul) creatures.

Nocturnal means "active at night."

51

Many nocturnal creatures have very large eyes. Their big eyes let in more light and help them see in the moonlit forest.

Night monkeys

Bats are common nocturnal creatures. There are hundreds of different kinds of bats in the world's rain forests. Many bats have a strong sense of smell that helps them find fruits and flowers in the dark.

Others use sound to find and capture insects and to find their way in the night.

Vampire bat

At night, rain forest trees twinkle with fireflies and click beetles. Scientists think insects like these "talk" to each other with their flashing lights.

Lucio firefly

Click beetle

Water Creatures

Rivers run through most of the rain forests of the world. Thousands of different kinds of fish live in these rivers. Snakes, crocodiles, and lizards slither and sleep on the banks.

Anacondas (an-uh-KON-duhz) attack animals that have come to the river for a drink of water.

54

Some rain forest
crocodiles are over
twenty feet long.

Flesh-eating piranha have
scary, razor-sharp teeth.
But they mostly eat berries,
fruits, seeds, and other fish.

Turn the page to meet more incredible
creatures of the rain forest.

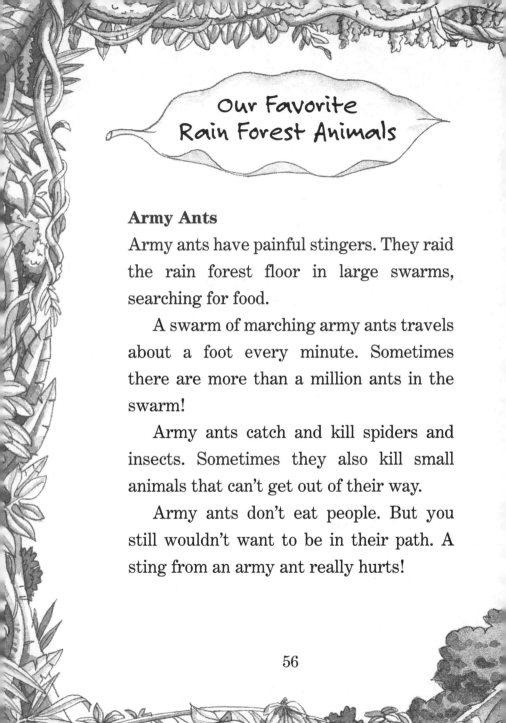

Our Favorite Rain Forest Animals

Army Ants

Army ants have painful stingers. They raid the rain forest floor in large swarms, searching for food.

A swarm of marching army ants travels about a foot every minute. Sometimes there are more than a million ants in the swarm!

Army ants catch and kill spiders and insects. Sometimes they also kill small animals that can't get out of their way.

Army ants don't eat people. But you still wouldn't want to be in their path. A sting from an army ant really hurts!

Army ants live in rain forests in South America.

57

Bird-eating tarantulas don't eat birds very often. They are much more likely to eat frogs, snakes, mice, and lizards.

58

Bird-Eating Tarantula
(Goliath spider)

The bird-eating tarantula (tuh-RAN-chuh-luh) is one of the biggest spiders in the world. A bird-eating tarantula can be eleven inches from the tip of one leg to another. That's bigger than a baseball glove!

Bird-eating tarantulas have sharp, curved fangs. Their fangs can be over an inch long!

Bird-eating tarantulas live in the rain forests of South America.

Queen Alexandra's Birdwing Butterfly

The Queen Alexandra's birdwing is the biggest butterfly in the world. This butterfly has a wingspan a foot wide!

The Queen Alexandra's birdwing is beautiful but dangerous. It is poisonous to eat. Creatures who eat it get very sick but do not usually die.

The Queen Alexandra's birdwing is very rare. It lives only in a small area of rain forest in New Guinea.

61

Goliath Beetle

Imagine an insect as big as a mouse, with long horns and six sharp claws. That's the Goliath (guh-LY-uth) beetle of the African rain forest.

The Goliath beetle is the heaviest insect in the world. It can weigh as much as a small hamster. It can be four inches long.

Goliath beetles have two sharp hooks on each of their six legs. They use these hooks to clamp on to the sides of trees. Once a Goliath beetle has attached itself to something, it's almost impossible to pull it off!

The Goliath beetle lives in the rain forests of Africa.

Red-Eyed Tree Frog

Red-eyed tree frogs eat mostly flies and other insects—but sometimes they eat other frogs!

Red-eyed tree frogs usually hunt at night. Their huge eyes help them see better in the dark. They have sticky fingers and toes that help them hold on to slippery tree trunks, branches, and leaves.

Red-eyed tree frogs lay their eggs in plants that hang over streams. When they hatch, the tadpoles plop right into the water!

Red-eyed tree frogs live in the rain forests of Central and South America.

Poison Arrow Frog

Poison arrow frogs are tiny—but deadly! Most poison arrow frogs are only an inch long. But they have a poison in their skin that is strong enough to kill anything that eats them. One poison arrow frog has enough poison to kill over a hundred people!

The bright colors of poison arrow frogs warn other animals that they are dangerous to eat. They got their name because for hundreds of years, hunters in the rain forest have used their poison on arrows and darts.

Poison arrow frogs live in the rain forests of Central and South America.

Sloth

Sloths are some of the slowest-moving creatures in the world. It could take a sloth over an hour to cross an average-sized living room!

Sloths have long, curved claws. Their claws look pretty scary. But sloths never attack other animals. They only eat leaves.

Sloths use their claws as hooks to hang on to tree branches. In fact, sloths live most of their lives hanging upside down.

Sloths live in the rain forests of Central and South America.

68

Toucan

There are about forty different kinds of toucans (TOO-kanz) in the rain forests of Central and South America.

Toucans have huge, colorful bills. They use their giant bills like scissors to snip berries and fruits from the branches of trees and bushes.

A toucan's bill isn't as heavy as it looks. It's a thin, hollow shell over a bony skeleton.

Toco toucan →

When toucans go to sleep, they turn their heads to the side and lay their bills on their backs. Then they fold their tails over their bills to cover them up.

Plate-billed mountain toucan

Toucans live in the rain forests of Central and South America.

Jaguar

Jaguars are beautiful big cats. Male jaguars can be six feet long and weigh 250–300 pounds. That's as big as a professional football player!

Jaguars are good climbers. They often

hide in rain forest trees, waiting to pounce on deer, wild pigs, or other animals that roam the forest floor.

Unlike most cats, jaguars are also good swimmers. They swim in rain forest rivers to catch fish, turtles—even crocodiles!

Sadly, there are few jaguars left in rain forests. Many have been killed off by hunters for their beautiful fur.

Jaguars live in the rain forests of Central and South America.

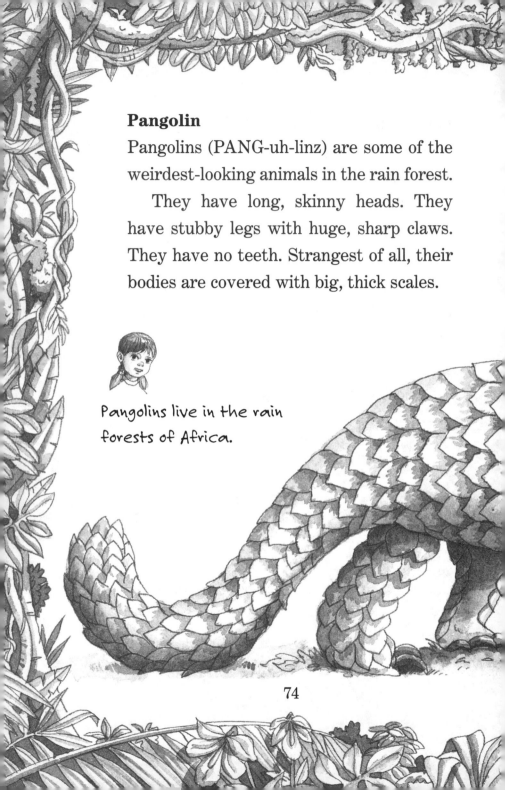

Pangolin

Pangolins (PANG-uh-linz) are some of the weirdest-looking animals in the rain forest.

They have long, skinny heads. They have stubby legs with huge, sharp claws. They have no teeth. Strangest of all, their bodies are covered with big, thick scales.

Pangolins live in the rain forests of Africa.

When a pangolin is scared, it rolls into a tight ball. Its scales protect it from any animal that tries to attack it.

Pangolins are sometimes called scaly anteaters. That's because ants are their favorite food. They usually go hunting for ants at night.

5
People of the Rain Forest

Thousands of people live in rain forests around the world. For centuries, they've gotten everything they've needed from the plants and animals of the forest.

Hunter-Gatherers

People of the rain forest usually live in small groups. Many get their food by hunting wild animals and gathering wild plants to eat. People who live this way are called *hunter-gatherers.*

The *Mbuti* (muh-BOO-tee) people are hunter-gatherers. They live deep in the Ituri Rain Forest of the Congo region of Africa.

The Mbuti hunt with spears and with bows and arrows. They also trap animals in large nets made from vines. They hunt antelopes, forest hogs, buffalo, elephants, monkeys, and other animals. They use the animal meat for food. They make tools and clothes from other parts of the animals. Almost nothing is wasted.

In the past, the Mbuti killed only what they needed for themselves and their families. Today, they also trade with villagers who live on the edge of the forest.

While Mbuti men hunt, women and children gather roots, nuts, fruits, snails, termites, and ants for food. Sometimes they catch fish or crabs.

The Mbuti move every few weeks to a new place in the forest, looking for wild animals and plants. The women and children set up the new camp. They build huts from branches and large leaves. They can build a whole village of huts in just a few hours.

Mbuti huts are shaped like beehives. There's only enough room for a few people to sleep inside.

The Mbuti make beautiful paintings on cloth made from bark. Men collect the bark from trees. They soften it with water and pound it with a hammer. The women then paint designs on the bark. Sometimes they paint pictures of forest creatures.

Mbuti bark-cloth painting.

Music is also an important part of Mbuti life. The Mbuti play rattles and drums. They sing when they hunt, gather honey, set up a new home, or play games.

The Mbuti use art and music as a way to honor the guardian spirit of the forest. The Mbuti believe the forest spirit is like a parent who watches over them and protects them. For this reason, they call themselves "children of the forest." Every day, they thank the forest for all the gifts it gives them.

Hunter-Gardeners

Some rain forest people get their food by raising crops as well as by hunting and gathering from the forest. People who live this way are sometimes called *hunter-gardeners*.

Hunter-gardeners clear land for their crops by cutting down trees and burning them. Then they plant seeds in the ashes of the burned trees. The ashes make the soil better for growing plants.

Hunter-gardeners usually grow their crops in the same place for only a few years. Then they move their field to another place, so that the rain forest trees and plants have a chance to grow back. It might be twenty years before they plant in the same place again.

The *Yanomami* (ya-nuh-MAH-mee) people are hunter-gardeners. They tend small gardens in the Amazon Rain Forest. They grow bananas, yams, and sweet potatoes. They also grow plantains, which are like large, tough bananas. They roast the plantains on coals or boil them in pots.

Besides growing their crops, the Yanomami gather nuts, mushrooms, and honey. They also hunt birds and catch frogs and insects to eat.

Yanomami boys learn to hunt at a very young age.

For shelter, the Yanomami build large huts made from tree branches and palm leaves. They build their huts in a large circle. In the evening, families come together inside the circle and tell stories. The Yanomami especially like to tell stories about jaguars, the most feared animals in the forest.

For many centuries, the Yanomami lived as their ancestors had lived. They had very little contact with people from the outside world. But recently all that changed.

In the 1980s, gold was discovered along the border between Brazil and Venezuela. This is the area where the Yanomami have lived for centuries. Thousands of people from outside the forest invaded Yanomami lands to mine the gold.

The gold miners have upset Yanomami life by cutting down trees and building roads. Their noisy planes and equipment have scared away animals. The miners have also introduced new diseases to the Yanomami, such as malaria, flu, and measles.

Governments of South American countries are now trying to protect the Yanomami people and their land.

Like the Mbuti, the Yanomami have lived for many years in peace with the rain forest. They believe that nature creates everything, and that people should love and respect the forest.

Rain forest people like the Yanomami

and the Mbuti have many things to teach those who live outside the rain forest. They can share their knowledge about which plants are good to eat, which are poisonous, and which are good for medicine.

Most important, the peoples of the rain forest can teach others how to take what is needed from the forest without destroying it.

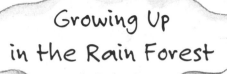

Growing Up
in the Rain Forest

Rain forest children learn a lot growing up in the forest. Here are some of their lessons:

1. *What to eat.*

Some rain forest plants and animals are poisonous. Rain forest children learn what's good to eat, and what's dangerous.

2. *How to hunt, gather, and cook.*

Girls learn to find good plants to eat and how to cook them.

Boys learn to hunt animals with spears, bows and arrows, and nets.

3. *How to have fun!*

Most rain forest people tell stories together at the end of the day. They sometimes dance and sing. Rain forest children learn the dances and songs and stories from their parents and other relatives.

6

Gifts of the Rain Forest

Rain forests can seem like magical, far-away places. But many things we use every day come from rain forests around the world.

Think about what you did yesterday. Did you eat a banana or a tomato? Bananas and tomatoes were first discovered in rain forests.

Did you sit on a chair or at a desk? You may have been sitting on the wood of a rain forest tree.

Did you ride in a car or bus, or on a bicycle? Tires are made of rubber. Rubber was first made from the sap of a tree found in rain forests.

Draining sap from a rubber tree doesn't hurt the tree.

Foods from the Rain Forest

Many food products originally came from rain forests. These foods and spices are so familiar to us now that we can hardly imagine a world without them. They include oranges, pineapples, grapefruits, avocados, black pepper, cinnamon, nutmeg, vanilla, coffee, peanuts, cashew nuts, chicle (the stuff that makes chewing gum chewy), and cocoa beans (used to make chocolate).

Many of these food products are now grown on large farms. But all were first found in rain forests around the world.

Cacao tree pods have cocoa beans inside.

Rain Forest Medicine

Another very important gift of the rain forest is medicine. For thousands of years, rain forest people have treated sickness with rain forest plants. Now scientists all over the world study the plants of the rain forest to find treatments for disease.

Rosy periwinkle

The rosy periwinkle is a flower that grows in rain forests in Africa. It is used in medicines that treat several kinds of

94

cancer. Other rain forest plants produce medicines for heart disease, high blood pressure, and stomach problems.

Scientists hope they will someday discover cures for AIDS and other terrible diseases in rain forest plants.

Global Warming

The rain forests of the world are important in another way. They help control the earth's climate.

Climate is the usual weather of a place.

The air around the earth is called the *atmosphere* (AT-mus-feer). The earth's atmosphere is filled with different kinds of gases. One of these gases is *oxygen* (AHK-sih-jun). Humans and animals need oxygen to breathe.

Another kind of gas in the atmosphere is *carbon dioxide* (KAR-bun dy-AHK-side). Carbon dioxide helps the atmosphere hold heat from the sun. But many scientists believe too much carbon dioxide can cause a problem. It can make the earth too hot. Scientists call this problem *global warming.*

Trees and plants need carbon dioxide to live and grow. The millions of rain forest trees and plants take huge amounts of carbon dioxide out of the atmosphere. In this way, they help protect our planet and all its creatures from global warming. This might be the rain forests' greatest gift of all.

Gifts of the Rain Forest
Food

Wood

Rubber

Medicine

Protection from global warming

Future Gifts

Scientists have studied only a small number of the plants and animals of the rain forest. There are many valuable things yet to be discovered.

Different kinds of fruits, nuts, and other foods from the rain forest might help feed the world's people. New kinds of medicines may be found in rain forest plants that haven't been discovered yet. Even new kinds of fuel for homes and cars might be found.

As long as rain forests keep growing and thriving, they will have endless gifts to give to the world.

7

Saving the Rain Forests

Rain forests are one of the earth's most valuable resources. But the rain forests of the world are in danger. They are being destroyed very quickly.

People are cutting down huge numbers of trees without replanting them. They're clearing large areas of land to build roads and houses. They're also clearing land to grow crops and raise cattle.

Half of the world's rain forests have

already been lost. Every second, an area of rain forest the size of a baseball field is destroyed.

Every rain forest is home to some plants and animals that live nowhere else in the world. When a forest is destroyed, these plants and animals are destroyed with it.

Environmentalists
The natural world is sometimes called the *environment* (en-VY-urn-munt). People who study the natural world and work to protect it are called *environmentalists* (en-VY-urn-MEN-tul-ists).

Environmentalists are working with governments in countries that have rain forests. They are also working with forest people and learning from them. They are trying to find ways to help the world get what it needs from rain forests without destroying them.

Nature Reserves

Nature reserves are places where land is protected by the government. Humans are not allowed to harm the animals and plants in a nature reserve. There are now nature reserves in rain forests all over the world.

Endangered Species

Some rain forest animals are becoming very rare. For example, there were once thousands of woolly spider monkeys in South American rain forests. Now there are only several hundred.

When an animal like the woolly spider monkey is in danger of dying out completely, it is said to be an *endangered species*. There are laws all over the world against killing endangered species. Sadly, many people ignore these laws. If the last animal of an endangered species dies, that kind of animal becomes *extinct*. It is gone from the earth forever.

Nearly 95 percent of the woolly spider monkeys' forest home has been destroyed.

How Kids Can Help

The more people know about rain forests, the more they care about them—and the harder they will work to protect them.

One of the best things *you* can do to save the rain forests is to *learn* about them. Then share what you learn with your friends and family. Tell them about the wonderful gifts of the rain forests. Tell them about the amazing plants and animals that live there. Tell them how important rain forests are to our planet.

In this way, kids everywhere can help protect and save these wonderful worlds.

Doing More Research

There's a lot more you can learn about rain forests and the amazing people, plants, and animals that live in them. The fun of research is seeing how many different sources you can explore.

Books

Most libraries and bookstores have lots of books about rain forests.

Here are some things to remember when you're using books for research:

1. You don't have to read the whole book. Check the table of contents and the index to find the topics you're interested in.

2. Write down the name of the book.

When you take notes, make sure you write down the name of the book in your notebook so you can find it again.

3. Never copy exactly from a book.

When you learn something new from a book, put it in your own words.

4. Make sure the book is <u>nonfiction</u>.

Some books tell make-believe stories of rain forest adventures. Make-believe stories are called *fiction*. They're fun to read, but not good for research.

Research books have facts and tell true stories. They are called *nonfiction*. A librarian or teacher can help you make sure the books you use for research are nonfiction.

Here are some good nonfiction books about rain forest plants, animals, and people:

- *Explore the Tropical Rain Forest* by Linda Tagliaferro

- *Nature's Green Umbrella* by Gail Gibbons

- *Rain Forest,* a DK Eye Wonder book

- *Rain Forests* by Richard C. Vogt

- *Tropical Rain Forest,* One Small Square series, by Donald M. Silver

- *Welcome to the Green House* by Jane Yolen

Zoos and Museums

Many zoos and natural history museums have rain forest exhibits. These exhibits can teach you a lot about rain forests and how important they are for the environment.

When you go to one of these exhibits:

1. Be sure to take your notebook!
Write down anything that catches your interest. Draw pictures, too!

2. Ask questions.
There are almost always people at museums and zoos who can help you find what you're looking for.

3. Check the calendar.
Many museums and zoos have special events and activities just for kids!

Here are some zoos and museums with rain forest exhibits:

- Denver Zoo
- Discovery Place (Charlotte, North Carolina)
- Indianapolis Zoo
- Little Rock Zoo (Arkansas)
- Moody Gardens (Galveston, Texas)
- San Diego Zoo

DVDs

There are some great nonfiction DVDs about life in the rain forest. As with books, make sure the DVDs you watch for research are nonfiction!

Check your library or video store for these and other nonfiction titles about rain forests:

- *Bugs! A Rainforest Adventure* from Image Entertainment

- *Jeff Corwin Experience: Guyana: A Rain Forest Ecosystem* from Discovery School

- *Let's Explore . . . the Rainforest* from One Smart Cookie Productions

The Internet

Many websites have facts about rain forests. Some also have games and activities that can help make learning about these amazing places even more fun.

Ask your teacher or your parents to help you find more websites like these:

- abcteach.com/directory/basics/science /habitats_biomes/rain_forest

- blueplanetbiomes.org/rainforest.htm

- childrenoftheearth.org/rainforest-for -kids.html

- ehow.com/list_7588344_rain-forest -plants-animals-kids.html

- hilozoo.com/zoo_facts_animals.php

- kids.nationalgeographic.com/kids/photos /tropical-rainforests/

- library.thinkquest.org/27257 /rainintro.html

- rainforest-alliance.org/kids

- rain-tree.com/schoolreports.htm

Good luck!

Index

Have you read the adventure that
matches up with this book?

Don't miss Magic Tree House® #6

Afternoon on the Amazon

When the magic tree house whisks
Jack and Annie to the Amazon River, it's not
long before they get hopelessly lost. Will they
be stuck in the rain forest forever?

If you like Magic Tree House® #46:
Dogs in the Dead of Night,
you'll love finding out the facts
behind the fiction in

Magic Tree House® Fact Tracker

DOG HEROES

A nonfiction companion to
Dogs in the Dead of Night

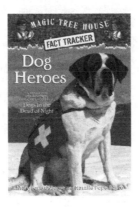

It's Jack and Annie's very own guide
to dog heroes!

Available now!

Magic Tree House® Books

Magic Tree House® Fact Trackers

More Magic Tree House®